AMAZING MILITARY MACHINES

MILITARY
DRONES AND ROBOTS

by Mari Schuh

PEBBLE
a capstone imprint

Published by Pebble, an imprint of Capstone.
1710 Roe Crest Drive, North Mankato, Minnesota 56003
capstonepub.com

Library of Congress Cataloging-in-Publication Data is available on the
Library of Congress website.
ISBN 9781666350296 (hardcover)
ISBN 9781666350333 (paperback)
ISBN 9781666350371 (ebook pdf)

Summary: Militaries use robots and drones in the air, on the ground,
and underwater all around the world. Drones spy on targets and
robots disable bombs to get the job done!

Image Credits
Alamy/agefotostock, 9; Getty Images: Riccardo Niccoli/Stocktrek
Images, 11; Newscom: Christian Charisius/dpa/picture-alliance,
15, NICOLAS NICOLAS MESSYASZ/SIPA, 17; Shutterstock:
BlueBarronPhoto, 4, Fafarumba, 21, nuttakit, 20 (notebook), studiovin,
20 (pencil); U.S. Air Force photo by Senior Airman Miranda Mahoney,
7, Tech. Sgt. Kevin J. Gruenwald, 5, Tech. Sgt. Matthew Lotz, Cover;
U.S. Army photo by Pfc. Nathan Goodall, 13, Sgt. Giancarlo Casem, 19,
Staff Sgt. Christopher Jelle, 18; U.S. Marine Corps photo by Sgt. Andy
O. Martinez, 12

Editorial Credits
Editor: Erika L. Shores; Designer: Dina Her; Media Researcher: Jo Miller;
Production Specialist: Tori Abraham

All internet sites appearing in back matter were available and accurate
when this book was sent to press.

Printed and bound in the USA. PO4882

TABLE OF CONTENTS

Words in **bold** are in the glossary.

NO PILOT ON BOARD

What is flying in the sky? It looks like an airplane. But no pilot is on board. It's a **drone**!

Militaries use drones and other **robots** for many jobs. They are used in the air, on land, and in water.

Troops on the ground can use **remote controls** to move these vehicles. Drones are also **programmed** to move on their own.

BLACK HORNET

The Black Hornet is a tiny drone. Troops can carry it with them. It can fly for 25 minutes. Wind and light rain do not stop it from taking photos and videos.

Who is around the corner? What is in the dark cave? This drone can find out while troops stay in a safe area.

MQ-1 PREDATOR

This drone is large and powerful. Its long wings stretch 66 feet (20 meters) wide. This helps the Predator reach 50,000 feet (15,240 m) high in the sky.

Flying over land and water, the Predator gathers information. Long **missions** are no problem. It can fly for 27 hours.

ANKA

The ANKA is a large drone with long,
narrow wings. It goes on long missions.
The ANKA can fly for 30 hours. It flies
in all kinds of weather.

If there are problems and the drone can't
get messages from the pilots, that's OK.
It is programmed to come back and land
all on its own.

RAVEN

Many troops use the Raven. This drone is small and light. It fits in a backpack. The drone does not fly very high. But it can fly for an hour and a half.

A battery gives the Raven its power.
But how does it start to fly? Troops throw
it into the air like a model airplane.

REMUS

Drones are also used under the sea. REMUS use **sonar** to search the ocean floor for **mines**. They also make maps of the ocean floor. A propeller and fins help these vehicles dive and steer in the water.

THEMIS

THeMIS is a drone that travels on land. Troops on the ground have lots of gear. THeMIS helps out. It carries heavy supplies and equipment.

It gets power from a battery or an engine. Two strong rubber tracks help it move on rough land. It travels through forests too.

TALON

TALON robots have been used around the world. They help keep troops safe. They disable bombs and other devices. Cameras on the robots give troops a good view of the ground.

TALON robots are rugged. They can go over piles of dirt, sand, and rock. They move through snow. They even climb stairs.

DESIGN YOUR OWN DRONE

If you could design your own drone, what would it look like? How would it be different from the drones we have today? What size would it be? What features would it have? Draw a picture of your drone.

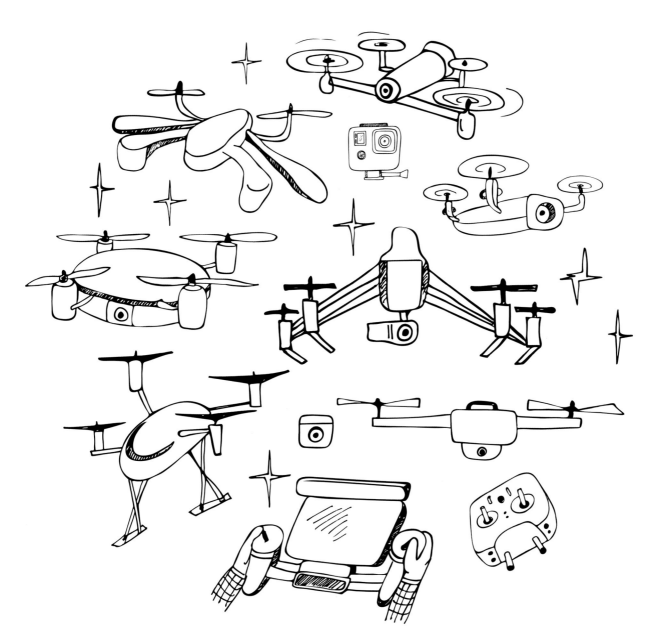

GLOSSARY

drone (DROHN)—an unmanned vehicle that is controlled by remote control or by computers on the vehicle

mine (MINE)—a type of bomb

mission (MISH-uhn)—a planned job or task

programmed (PROH-gramd)—to have entered a series of step-by-step instructions into a computer, drone, robot, or vehicle that tells it what to do

remote control (ri-MOHT kuhn-TROHL)—a device used to control machines from a distance

robot (ROH-bot)—a machine programmed to do different jobs

sonar (SOH-nar)—a device that uses sound waves to find underwater objects

READ MORE

Faust, Daniel R. *Drones for the Police and Military.* New York: PowerKids Press, 2020.

Murray, Julie. *Drones.* Minneapolis: Abdo Zoom, a division of ABDO, 2021.

Schaefer, Lola. *Flying Robots.* Minneapolis: Lerner Publications, 2021.

INTERNET SITES

Drone Facts
softschools.com/facts/technology/drones_facts/3355/

Drones to the Rescue
kidsdiscover.com/teacherresources/drones-uavs-rescue/

Robot Facts for Kids
kids.kiddle.co/Robot

INDEX

ABOUT THE AUTHOR

Mari Schuh's love of reading began with cereal boxes at the kitchen table. Today, she is the author of hundreds of nonfiction books for beginning readers. Mari lives in the Midwest with her husband and their sassy house rabbit. Learn more about her at marischuh.com.